What's the Attraction?

Written by Mary-Anne Creasy

Flying Start
to Literacy®

Contents

Introduction

If you could holiday anywhere in the world, where would you go and what would you most like to do? Do you like to do nothing but relax? Or do you want an adventure, or something new, that you haven't experienced before?

People have always travelled. Not so long ago, people travelled mainly to find work, visit family, or move to a new place and start a new life. But today, many people travel when they go on holiday – they travel for pleasure and excitement.

Most people travel within their own country – they don't need a passport, everyone speaks the same language and it's easier. But more and more people are travelling to other countries and experiencing different cultures.

In 1990, there were 435 million international tourists. In 2018, there were 1.4 *billion* – that's more than three times as many people travelling internationally in just 30 years.

Popular places

The most popular country to visit is France, followed by Spain and then the United States. And what's the most popular single destination to visit? According to one source, it is the Empire State Building in New York City, in the United States.

Chapter 1

Built for tourists

What sort of holiday would you like best? Maybe you like the idea of staying at a place where you can eat, sleep and play without leaving?

If so, then resorts, theme parks or cruises may be just right for you! They ensure that everything you need is in the one place.

Resorts

Resorts are built specifically for people on holiday. They have everything you need for a fun and relaxing stay – accommodations, swimming pools and restaurants. Many have shops, golf courses, gyms and even their own beaches.

You can do activities together as a family, like snorkelling, windsurfing or playing beach volleyball. Some resorts have special clubs just for kids. At these kids' clubs, you can make jewellery, play minigolf or go hiking.

Resorts provide such great service and attention, many guests want to stay longer. This type of holiday relieves the pressure of travelling, looking for activities, searching for somewhere to eat and then finding somewhere to stay.

Theme parks

What if you want to have a holiday experience that is all about fun and entertainment?

Theme parks have rides and other entertainment, and they cater to guests of all ages. There are slow rides for young children or those who don't seek big, fast thrills. There are also shows to entertain, games to play, and so many things to see and do, you could never be bored.

Some theme parks are watery playgrounds, which are great to visit on hot summer days. You can cool off in pools and waterfalls. And if you want something more thrilling, giant slippery slides spin and slip you through tunnels and down funnels until you splash into a pool at the end.

My theme park experience

When I was 12, I went with my parents to
one of the biggest theme parks in the world.
It was mind-bogglingly big – the parking lots
alone were so big, you had to get a bus and a monorail to
get through them. It was as if you were visiting a hundred
different places all in one day: one minute we were in a
huge treehouse and the next a rainforest jungle – that is
after a long time waiting in a queue.

I remember things were happening around us all the time –
music came from every angle, even the trees and flowerbeds
were singing to us, and there were parades every few hours,
including fireworks displays during the day! Every ride told
a story: a rollercoaster wasn't just a rollercoaster,
it included a tale told by animatronics and music.

The park is designed to ensure that you are
entertained at every possible moment,
but this also meant for me that it was
an overwhelmingly exhausting place
to spend the day. When given the
choice to return the next day, I chose
to spend it in the hotel pool!

Cruises

Cruises are another way of holidaying in one place. Cruise ships are like floating resorts with thousands of passengers. Once you buy your ticket, everything is included – accommodations, meals (including drinks) and entertainment.

On a cruise holiday, you spend most of your time at sea. There are lots of activities – extreme waterslides, rock climbing and go-karting on deck are just some of the many activities for you to try. The cruise ship delivers you to different destinations on your **itinerary**, where you can take daytrips to see the sights. There is no packing and unpacking, or checking in and out at each stop.

Cruise holidays are wonderful for the people on the ship, but what about some of the small towns and villages they visit? When a cruise ship docks at a destination for a day, thousands of passengers flood into the town or village. They don't stay long, and they don't spend much money on food and accommodations because almost everything they need is provided by the cruise ship.

Chapter 2

Natural wonders

The world is full of natural wonders – bright coral reefs teeming with fish, mountains topped with snow, deep, rocky canyons and lush rainforests.

Two popular natural attractions that people love to visit are Uluru in Australia and Hawaii Volcanoes National Park in the United States.

Milford Sound

Milford Sound in the Fjordland National Park, New Zealand, attracts tourists from all over the world. They come to hike, go kayaking or just gaze at the spectacular steep landscape.

Niagara Falls

More than 30 million people visit Niagara Falls in New York State each year. Most visitors walk along the specially built walkways near the falls for a great view. To get up close to the falls, you can take a boat ride – but make sure you wear a raincoat!

Uluru, Central Australia

Uluru is one of the most famous landmarks in Australia and a sacred site of the Anangu (arn-ung-oo) people who have lived there for 30,000 years.

For many years, tourists were able to climb the rock, which was a risky activity because it was easy to slip and fall. But in 2019, the rock was closed permanently to climbers out of respect for the Anangu people and their wishes that their sacred site not be climbed.

There are many other ways to see Uluru: you can walk around it, hop on a Segway or even take a camel ride. The nine-kilometre track around the rock takes you through beautiful scenery where you can admire the enormous shapes, textures and caves of the huge **monolith**. Just remember to take plenty of water and finish your walk by 11 o'clock in the morning, before the heat of the day makes it too dangerous to exercise. The spectacular rock is a photographer's dream as it changes colour throughout the day. It is best seen at sunrise and sunset when it glows orange and red.

Tourists who would like to learn more about the Anangu people and their culture can take art classes using traditional techniques or hear stories about the meaning and importance of Uluru.

Hawaii Volcanoes National Park

The island of Hawaii is famous around the world for its huge waves. But it also has another natural attraction, one that includes an element of danger – Hawaii Volcanoes National Park. Visitors can explore the incredible variety of landscapes, including lush rainforests and caves of cooled lava. They can also hike around the most exciting part of the park: the volcanoes.

The park contains two of the world's most active volcanoes, Kilauea (Keel-ow-ay-ah) and Mauna Loa. In May 2018, Kilauea volcano erupted, with ash exploding into the air and lava flowing at speeds of more that 30 kilometres an hour, burying roads and destroying hundreds of homes. Nearly 2,000 people were **evacuated** from the area.

To keep visitors safe, the park was closed. But this only made some people more eager to get closer to the volcano so they could take exciting photos. Some people even climbed over **barricades** to take selfies of the hot lava as it flowed, unaware that even breathing in the gas from the lava was dangerous.

When the volcano finally stopped erupting in late 2018, the park reopened. It remains the most popular place to visit on the island of Hawaii because of the thrill of being close to the ever-present danger of the volcanoes.

Chapter 3

Seasonal attractions

Some people like to visit places for their natural attractions. But because nature changes all the time, some of these attractions can be seen only at certain times of the year.

For a brief few weeks, or even just a few days, animals migrate, wildflowers bloom and leaves change colour. Nature lovers are attracted to these spectacular seasonal displays, and there are a lot of nature lovers!

Pink wildflowers, Western Australia

Wildflowers

In parts of Western Australia, from June until December, millions of flowers spring up and carpet the ground. It is one of the largest wildflower blooms on Earth with more than 12,000 different species to be found – nearly 70 per cent are not found anywhere else.

Tourists use a website to guide them to the best spots so they avoid being disappointed. The website has a "wildflower track" of photos that people have posted with the date and location. The website also reminds visitors to never pick the flowers or they will get a $2,000 fine!

Thousands of visitors go to see this spectacular display of colour each year. Most people drive, but there are also bus tours, cycling tours or guided walking tours. Some people even take scenic flights in small planes to view the huge carpet of colour across the landscape.

Western Australia is a vast place and many remote areas don't have a lot of accommodation so during the wildflower season be sure to book ahead.

Autumn leaves

For only a few weeks each year, some people are lucky enough to see another spectacular natural sight. In southeastern Australia and southern New Zealand during autumn, the **foliage** on the trees begins to change from green to yellow, gold, orange and red. For a few weeks, the trees are a brilliant blaze of colour before their leaves turn brown and fall off.

During this time, millions of people travel in buses and cars along the country roads, sometimes stopping to take photos.

Lake Hayes, New Zealand

Tourists have maps that show the best places to see the most amazing leaf colours, and the most popular areas are those that are in peak colour.

For the locals, however, it can be frustrating when they get caught up in a slow-moving traffic jam caused by the tourists. But towns and villages in the region have learnt to embrace the popularity of the season. Each year, they hold fairs and festivals in autumn to promote their area and to encourage the tourists to enjoy events other than driving around to look at trees.

Chapter 4

Wonderful cities

You might live in a city and think it's an ordinary place, with nothing special to see. So why would anyone want to visit your hometown?

But many people live in cities that are tourist attractions because they are particularly beautiful or because they have interesting buildings and other places to visit.

A pedestrian bridge over a canal, Venice

The Grand Canal, Venice

Venice, Italy

Venice is an ancient city built on a **lagoon**, with a history dating back more than 1,500 years. It has been described as "the most beautiful city in the world". It is such an important city that it is protected by the United Nations because of its buildings and art. Even the smallest buildings in Venice have paintings by some of history's most important artists.

All these qualities make Venice a place many people would like to visit at least once. Apart from its important and beautiful monuments, palaces, squares and churches, this city is built on more than a hundred small islands connected by 400 bridges. There are no roads or cars, only canals and narrow, winding streets. People walk, ride bikes, or take water buses or water taxis to explore the city.

Today, tourism is the main industry in Venice. Tourists have been visiting Venice for hundreds of years, but in the past 20 years, the number of people visiting the city has exploded.

Venice is also a destination for cruise ships that arrive daily, carrying thousands of visitors. Tourists, which now number nearly 30 million each year, often make this small, historic city – with only 60,000 residents – a very crowded place.

My week in Venice

One summer, sweaty and jet-lagged after our long flight from Australia, my family and I caught our first glimpse of the "Floating City". As we precariously perched atop a water taxi – racing away from the airport – the wind's blustering was a welcome relief. The next week was spent exploring narrow streets, strolling across bridges and lounging in the small apartment that overlooked a canal. Making scones with my English nana in that small Italian kitchen is a memory I cherish.

When we were in Venice, there was a famous art exhibition. I loved walking along the canals and over the bridges to get to the island where we saw paintings and sculptures from around the world.

On our last night, we went on a stargazing gondola voyage – it was just like magic. Venice is a city bustling with energy – it's hard not to love.

Canberra, Australian Capital Territory

Nearly more than 100 years ago, a young American architect won a competition to design Canberra, and the result today is a city that looks like a huge park. There are wide tree-lined streets, an artificial lake and of course many large buildings, monuments and cultural centres.

Canberra, the capital of Australia, is where the Australian Federal Government meets and passes laws in Parliament House. You can watch politicians debate each other in the Public Galleries.

For an unforgettable day, visit the Australian War Memorial, a museum of the country's involvement in many conflicts around the world. Canberra is also home to many other important places like the National Museum of Australia and the High Court of Australia.

My visit to Canberra

When I went to Canberra, I learnt a lot – not only about Australian history, but also about how those events are remembered and honoured today. The scale of the War Memorial was impressive. I saw warplanes, helicopters and submarines, and I could hear the noises these huge machines make during an amazing sound and light effects show.

I also really liked the National Science and Technology Centre – Questacon. I liked the giant "Free Fall" slide that lets you experience the force of gravity. Next time I visit, I would like to go to Parliament House.

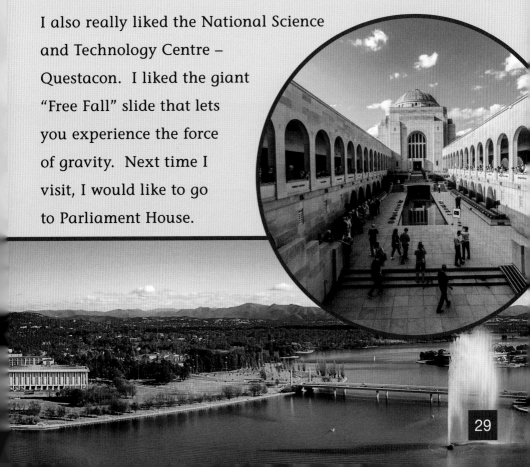

Conclusion

Today, there are so many places to go and things to do that it can be difficult to decide on where to spend your holiday!

Do you want to see nature at its most colourful best – or to explore its magnificent, awe-inspiring wonders? Or are you eager to visit and admire an important or historical city that will surprise and educate you? Then again, you can opt for a holiday just to have fun, be entertained or simply enjoy being away from home.

Glossary

barricades walls or fences that are put in place to stop people from entering

evacuated to be removed from a place that is dangerous or could become dangerous

foliage the leaves on plants

itinerary the places to be visited on a journey

lagoon an area of water that is separated by a sandbar from a larger body of water such as a sea or ocean

monolith a huge single stone

Index